FOCUS ON

ROMANS

ANITA GANERI

SHOOTING STAR PRESS

INTRODUCTION

The story of the Roman Empire begins with its growth from a group of tiny villages into one of the world's greatest empires, and ends with its collapse. At its height, the Empire controlled half of Europe, much of the Middle East, and parts of North Africa. This book provides the historical background to the Roman Empire, and links it with information about language and literature, science and math projects, geographical facts, and art activities. The key below shows how these subjects are divided up. We hope that the following projects will help you to develop your own ways of discovering the world of the Romans.

This edition produced in **1993** for
Shooting Star Press Inc
230 Fifth Avenue
New York, NY 10001

Design	David West Children's Book Design
Designer	Flick Killerby
Series Director	Bibby Whittaker
Editors	Fiona Robertson
	Elise Bradbury
Picture Research	Emma Krikler
Illustrators	Peter Kesteven
	Dave Burroughs
	David Russell

Created and produced by
Aladdin Books Ltd
28 Percy Street
London W1P 9FF

First published in the
United States in 1992 by
Gloucester Press

ISBN 1-56924-034-5

Printed in Belgium

Geography
The symbol of the planet earth shows where geographical facts and activities are included. These sections look at the extent of the Roman Empire at its height. Information is also given about the organization of a Roman town.

Language and literature
An open book is the sign for activities that involve language. These will explore how words are derived from the Latin language. Activities also involve looking at some Roman myths and legends.

Science and math

The microscope symbol indicates a science project or information, or a math project. Topics covered include how the Romans developed a system of central heating.

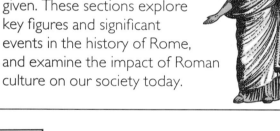

History

The sign of the scroll and hourglass shows where historical information is given. These sections explore key figures and significant events in the history of Rome, and examine the impact of Roman culture on our society today.

Social history

The symbol of a family shows where information about social history is given. These sections aim to provide an insight into the everyday lives of the Romans. Topics covered include what the Romans wore and what they ate.

Arts, crafts, and music

The symbol showing a sheet of music and art tools signals arts, crafts, or musical activities. There are many fun and imaginative ways of recreating Roman artifacts. Projects include making a theater mask, and creating your own mosaic.

CONTENTS

KINGDOM TO REPUBLIC 4/5

THE EARLY EMPIRE 6/7

THE ROMAN ARMY 8/9

ROMAN SOCIETY 10/11

THE PAX ROMANA 12/13

UNDER ROMAN RULE 14/15

BUILDING FEATS.................................16/17

RICH AND POOR 18/19

ENTERTAINMENT 20/21

GODS AND RELIGION.......................22/23

THE ROMAN LANGUAGE 24/25

THE END OF THE EMPIRE...................26/27

THE LEGACY OF ROME.....................28/29

DATE CHART...30/31

GLOSSARY...31

INDEX...32

KINGDOM TO REPUBLIC

Rome began as a group of villages built on seven hills beside the Tiber River in Italy. At first, it was ruled by kings. In 509 B.C., however, King Tarquin the Proud was driven out and Rome became a Republic. It was now governed by two consuls, elected each year by a law-making body, called the Senate (see page 14). By 266 B.C., Rome had overpowered its neighbors in Italy and begun its conquest abroad. By 50 B.C., it controlled most of the Mediterranean. But power struggles between rival army generals and tensions between rich and poor soon led to civil wars and unrest.

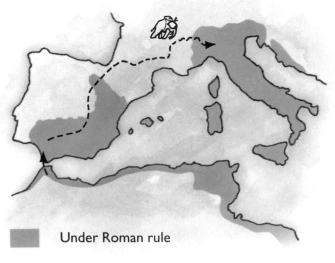

- Under Roman rule
- Under Carthaginian rule
- --→ Hannibal's route

The Punic Wars

Between 264-146 B.C., Rome waged war with Carthage, a powerful trading city in North Africa. In 218 B.C., the Carthaginian general Hannibal led an army of 35,000 men and 37 elephants over the Alps into Italy. However, Carthage was eventually defeated in 146 B.C.

Romulus and Remus

The traditional date for the founding of Rome is given as 753 B.C. Legend says that the city was founded by a man called Romulus. He and his twin brother, Remus, had been brought up by a she-wolf. The brothers later quarreled, Remus was killed and Romulus became the first king of Rome.

Civilizations

Greek civilization influenced many aspects of the developing Roman culture. Greek styles of art and architecture, such as those used in the Parthenon, below, were adapted by the Romans to suit their own purposes. The Romans also greatly admired Greek methods of teaching and education. Slaves were often brought to Rome from Greece to work as teachers. As the Romans grew more powerful, they in turn began to influence other civilizations.

The Parthenon in Athens, Greece

Julius Caesar

Julius Caesar was elected consul in 59 B.C. In 49 B.C., he defeated his rivals and seized power as a dictator. Caesar introduced social reform, but behaved too much like a king for many senators. On March 15, 44 B.C., he was murdered. Civil wars followed, leading to the downfall of the Republic.

The Julian calendar

Julius Caesar introduced the Julian calendar in 46 B.C. It is the basis of our modern calendar. Previously, the calendar had consisted of 355 days, divided into 12 months. To make the calendar more accurate, the Romans added 22 or 23 days every other year. But this system was not always followed correctly. Caesar added 90 days to the year 46 B.C. to bring his new calendar in line.

The festival of Saturnalia was the forerunner of Christmas. It took place in December.

Civil wars

The success of the Roman expansion abroad caused many problems in Rome itself. During the wars with Carthage, local farmers had been recruited into the army ranks, and their farms had suffered from neglect or military destruction. When the wars ended, the farmers could not afford to repair the damage, and were forced to give up their land to rich landowners. Many flocked to the cities, where they remained unemployed and poverty stricken. In Rome itself, leading citizens struggled for power, and the armies proved more loyal to their commanders than to the Senate. Civil wars erupted and the old republic crumbled.

THE EARLY EMPIRE

In 27 B.C., Julius Caesar's great-nephew, Octavian, emerged as the victor of the civil wars which had erupted after Caesar's death. Octavian restored peace and stability to Rome. He was anxious not to be thought of as a king – a title hated by the Romans – and established himself instead as Rome's first emperor, which was a military title. The Senate also gave him the title "Augustus" which means "revered" in Latin. Under his rule, every aspect of government was reformed, from the army to coinage to taxation, and many new cities were built. The period of Roman Empire, which was to last for the next 500 years, had begun.

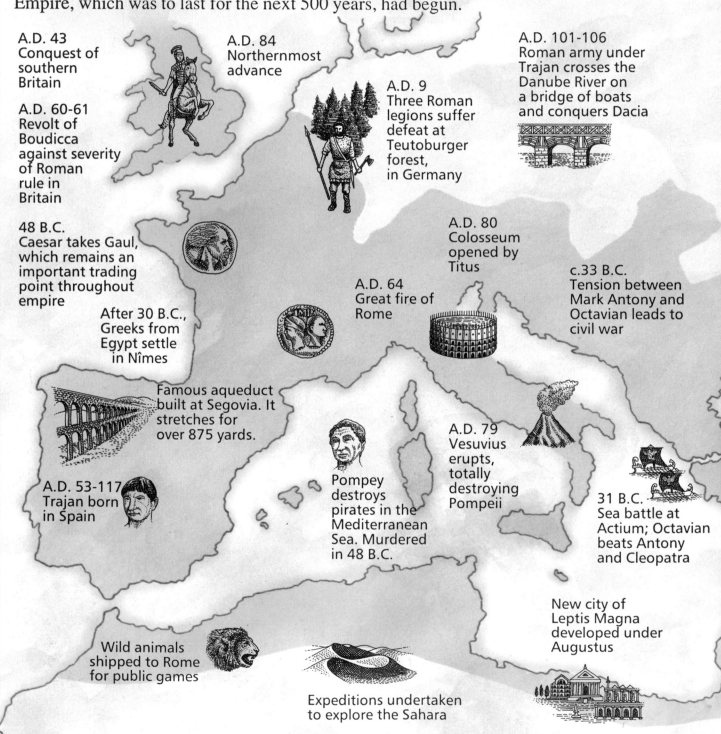

A.D. 43
Conquest of southern Britain

A.D. 60-61
Revolt of Boudicca against severity of Roman rule in Britain

48 B.C.
Caesar takes Gaul, which remains an important trading point throughout empire

After 30 B.C., Greeks from Egypt settle in Nîmes

Famous aqueduct built at Segovia. It stretches for over 875 yards.

A.D. 53-117
Trajan born in Spain

A.D. 84
Northernmost advance

A.D. 9
Three Roman legions suffer defeat at Teutoburger forest, in Germany

A.D. 80
Colosseum opened by Titus

A.D. 64
Great fire of Rome

Pompey destroys pirates in the Mediterranean Sea. Murdered in 48 B.C.

A.D. 79
Vesuvius erupts, totally destroying Pompeii

A.D. 101-106
Roman army under Trajan crosses the Danube River on a bridge of boats and conquers Dacia

c.33 B.C.
Tension between Mark Antony and Octavian leads to civil war

31 B.C.
Sea battle at Actium; Octavian beats Antony and Cleopatra

New city of Leptis Magna developed under Augustus

Wild animals shipped to Rome for public games

Expeditions undertaken to explore the Sahara

B.C. to A.D.

Yearly dates today are based on the birth of Christ. The years before His birth (B.C. means Before Christ) are counted backward. For example, Julius Caesar was murdered in 44 B.C. and Augustus became emperor 17 years later, in 27 B.C. The years after the birth of Christ are counted forward. A.D. stands for *anno Domini* (in the year of our Lord). Augustus died in A.D. 14. How many years did he rule for? (Note: A.D. 1 follows directly after 1 B.C.)

Importance of the countryside

Although the Roman Empire was famous for its magnificent cities, much of its wealth came from the countryside. Most people lived off the land, and farming was one of the empire's most important industries. Among the crops grown were grapes for making wine, and olives which were used for olive oil, as well as for eating. As the empire expanded, farming became more efficient and productive. Better equipment and new crops were introduced all over the empire. Many wealthy city dwellers loved the idea of a life in the countryside, and built lavish country villas.

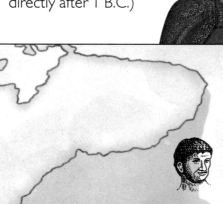

Diana of Ephesus

Garni, most easterly point, reached. Used as fortifications by Romans during campaigns of Nero

A.D. 70
Triumph over Jewish rebellion by Titus on behalf of his father, Vespasian

A.D. 73
Siege of Masada ends in the suicide of the defenders

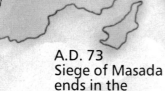

30 B.C.
Antony and his lover, the Egyptian Queen Cleopatra, commit suicide. Octavian becomes sole ruler of the Roman world

The first emperors

Augustus ruled from 27 B.C. until A.D. 14. He was

Augustus

succeeded by his stepson, Tiberius, who ruled until A.D. 37. Gaius (whose nickname was Caligula) was the next emperor. Caligula's extravagant life-style and his cruelty made him extremely unpopular, and he was murdered in A.D. 41. Tiberius's nephew, Claudius, ruled from A.D. 41-54. It is thought that he was poisoned by his fourth wife, Agrippina, so that her son by a previous marriage, Nero, could become Emperor.

Claudius

Nero

Nero killed himself in A.D. 68. There were then four rival candidates for the throne, which eventually passed in A.D. 69 to Vespasian, the founder of the Flavian dynasty. He was followed by Titus (A.D. 79-81), Domitian (A.D. 81-96) and Nerva (A.D. 96-98). The Spaniard, Trajan, ruled from A.D. 98-117, followed by Hadrian (A.D. 117-138).

Vespasian

Trajan

THE ROMAN ARMY

The rapid expansion and incredible success of the Roman Empire was largely due to the Roman army. It was first formed to defend the city of Rome, but it went on to conquer a vast empire. The early Roman army was made up of volunteers. General Marius (see below) reorganized it into a well trained and better equipped force. Soldiers became paid professionals who joined up for 20-25 years. People from lands conquered by the Romans were also recruited into the army ranks.

A legionary's uniform

Over a woolen tunic, a legionary wore a breast plate made of metal strips, scales, or rings. He also had a helmet of **Helmet** leather or metal. During cold weather, the thongs of his heavy, studded sandals were stuffed with wool and fur and he was given a thick, hooded cloak, called a *Birrus britannicus*, to keep him warm. A foot soldier was armed with a short sword, two metal-tipped javelins, and a rectangular shield of wood and leather. On the march, a legionary had to carry all his equipment on his back. Each man had a heavy pack which contained his tools, food, and so on. Fully-laden legionaries were nicknamed "Marius's mules" after the general and consul, Marius (157-86 B.C.).

Breast plate

Copy of shield

Tribune

Legatus

Emperor

Emperor   Legatus   Tribune   Centurion   Signifer   Legionary   Auxilary

The order of ranks in the Roman army is shown on the left. Senior offices, such as Legatus and Tribune, were usually held by members of the upper classes.

A Roman legion

A Roman legion was divided up into separate units. Ten sections of eight men made up a century. Six centuries made a cohort (480 men) and there were ten cohorts in a legion. There were also about 120 cavalrymen attached to each legion. Each legion had as its standard a silver eagle, the symbol of the Roman Empire.

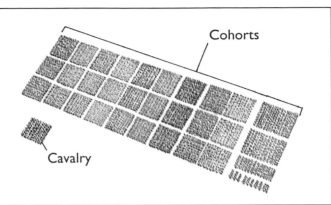

Cohorts

Cavalry

Signifer

Aquifer

Auxilary cavalry

Centurion

Praetorian guard

Fighting talk

Many of the words that we use today come from Latin.

A corduroy consisted of logs laid side by side to form the foundations of a rampart. The pattern of lines on corduroy cloth resembles the logs.

A praefectus was a high official in Rome. Today, the word prefect means someone with authority.

Gladius is the Latin word for sword. From it come the words gladiator and gladioli.

Ballista is the Latin word for catapult. Today the word ballistics is used in connection with weapons.

Tortoise technique

The Romans devised many new military techniques. The "tortoise" formation involved soldiers holding their shields above their heads as protection against arrows, stones, and other missiles hurled by the enemy. The raised shields resembled the pattern on a tortoise's shell and offered a similar type of protection, hence its name. The Romans also used assault towers and battering rams as a way of storming enemy territory.

ROMAN SOCIETY

Roman society was highly organized. People were divided into citizens and slaves. Citizens themselves were divided into different ranks, and had special rights and duties that were denied to noncitizens. They could vote in elections and serve in the army. But they were also expected to pay taxes. By A.D. 212 all free members of the empire were allowed to become Roman citizens.

Slaves had no such privileges. Many of them were prisoners of war. They were bought and sold by wealthy Romans who put them to work in their homes and estates.

The Senate and senators

The Senate was the main law- and policy-making body in Rome. During the Republic, the senators were members of aristocratic families. Two consuls were elected to head the Senate. Poorer citizens campaigned for and eventually won the right to stand for high office. The Senate continued to function under the Roman emperors.

The toga

The toga was a sign of Roman citizenship. Senators wore togas with a distinctive purple stripe.

Portraiture

Roman portraits were usually carved from marble, and were intended to be an accurate representation of the subject. Unattractive or unusual features, as well as beauty, were often emphasized.

The family

The family was ruled by a *paterfamilias* (father), who had complete authority over his wife, children, and slaves. When he died, each of his sons became head of a new family which was related to the old one by name. The resulting chain of families was known as a clan.

A Roman portrait of a man and his wife

Spartacus and the slaves

Slaves had no rights or status. They were owned by Roman citizens, or by the state. Many were treated very cruelly by their masters, and there were several rebellions by discontented slaves. The most famous was the one led by Spartacus, a gladiator. He formed an army of slaves in 73 B.C., which had over 90,000 members. Spartacus's army achieved several victories until its eventual defeat by the Roman army in 71 B.C.

Slaves revolt under Spartacus

Patricians and plebeians

There were three classes of Roman citizens. Patricians were the wealthiest and most aristocratic. They held most of the important political, religious, and legal appointments. Equites were rich business people. The ordinary citizens were called plebeians, or "commoners."

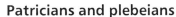

Slaves and freedmen

The Roman Empire relied heavily on slave labor. Slaves did most of the dirty jobs. But educated Greek slaves were highly valued as tutors and some became very influential. Some slaves were granted their freedom, or were allowed to buy it. They were known as freedmen.

The business classes

The period of early empire was one of great prosperity, in which trade flourished. A powerful middle class of businessmen, traders, and bankers had emerged, called equites. The equites were responsible for the wealth of goods that flooded into the empire (see map, right). Most of the bread eaten in Rome was made from Egyptian wheat, which arrived daily at the Roman ports in huge galleys. Luxury goods, such as spices, Indian cotton, and precious stones traveled to Rome by ship, and silks from China traveled along the Silk Road.

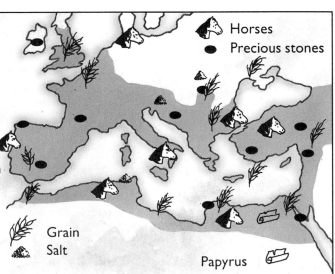

Horses

Precious stones

Grain
Salt

Papyrus

THE PAX ROMANA

Emperor Trajan ruled from A.D. 98-117. During his reign, the empire reached its greatest size with the conquest of large areas of land in the east. His successor, Hadrian, halted the spread and concentrated on improving the way the empire was run. This was the time of the Pax Romana, the Roman Peace, which was maintained by the army. People could travel and trade in safety, and new ideas, like Christianity, began to spread from the east.

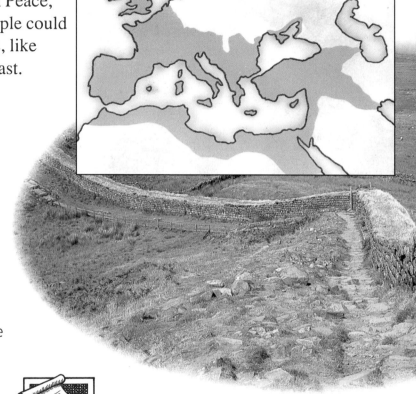

Hadrian

Hadrian ruled Rome from A.D. 117-138. He spent a great deal of his time touring the empire and decided that it had grown too large to be easily defended. So he gave up some of the latest conquests made by Trajan in the east and built fortifications along the most vulnerable frontiers (see opposite). He also reformed the administration of the empire and strengthened the army with local soldiers.

Coinage

The first Roman coin was used in about 280 B.C. Coins were originally minted to pay soldiers' wages and make the collection of taxes easier. Gradually, they began to be used all over the empire and replaced the bartering system in which people traded with goods, not money. As trade increased, merchants needed money to finance the growing network, and this led to the introduction of money-lending and banking. Under Augustus, all coins were given a fixed value. Coins were also issued to commemorate victories or mark special events in Rome's history.

The coin shown right was minted during Hadrian's reign.

Roman numerals

Roman numerals are written from left to right and added together to give a number. Thus, 2,650 is written MM (2,000), DC (500 + 100 = 600), L (50). Write out some other numerals.

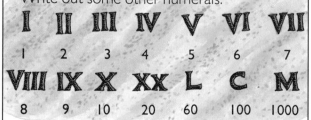

I	II	III	IV	V	VI	VII
1	2	3	4	5	6	7

VIII	IX	X	XX	L	C	M
8	9	10	20	60	100	1000

Fortified walls were built at Hadrian's command in Germany, Numidia in Africa, and Britain. The one in Britain (pictured below left) is known as Hadrian's Wall, and is the best preserved. The map (inset) shows the empire at its greatest extent. Roman provinces are marked in brown.

Making mosaics

Mosaics were made from tiny pieces of colored stone or tile, and used to decorate walls, floors, and sidewalks. They showed scenes from mythology or daily life, or abstract patterns. You can make a mosaic like the one below using paper, or modeling clay. On a large piece of paper, sketch the design you want to use. Cut out the different colors you need and glue them onto the design, working on one area at a time. Use tiny triangles and squares to give the effect of curved lines.

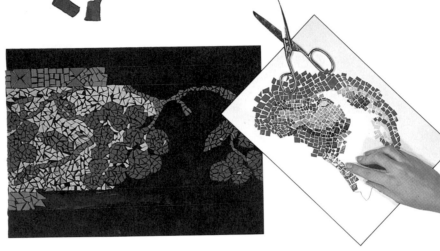

Medicine

The Romans gained much of their medical knowledge from the Greeks, and in particular from the Greek doctor Hippocrates. Roman medicine was a mixture of science and religion. Plants were used in medicines, and operations were also performed – without anesthetic. Ancient iron and bronze medical instruments (pictured) have been found. People also believed in the healing powers of the gods. Figures such as the one shown right of a woman with a spinal condition, were placed in temples of healing as offerings to the gods.

Central heating

The hypocaust system was a form of underfloor central heating which was invented in the first century A.D. Buildings were specially built with spaces between their inner and outer walls, and beneath the floors. A fire was lit and the heat was allowed to flow into the cavities. The hypocaust was used mainly to heat the bathhouses (see page 17), but in cold climates it could also be found in the villas of more wealthy citizens.

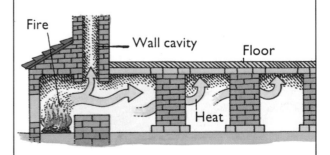

Fire / Wall cavity / Floor / Heat

UNDER ROMAN RULE

During the Republic, the Senate was the main law body in Rome (see page 10). In 450 B.C., however, the plebeians rebelled against the senators who held power. They demanded that the laws of Rome should be written down, so that new laws could not be invented and used against them. This body of law was called the Twelve Tables. During the Roman Empire, the emperor was the supreme ruler. Governors were elected from the Senate to oversee the provinces. The emperor was also the chief priest *(Pontifex Maximus)* of Rome.

The Justinian Code
The Twelve Tables listed laws governing ownership of property, family matters, types of punishments, and so on. They were constantly being added to. In A.D. 528, Emperor Justinian set about putting the huge mass of Roman law into order. His work became known as the Justinian Code. It became the basis of legal systems throughout the world, including the present system in France. Roman law is still studied as part of university law degrees all over the world.

As today, Roman criminals were tried by a jury. In serious cases, the jury consisted of up to 75 citizens and a lawyer was appointed to represent the accused person. Trials were held in huge government buildings, called basilicas. It was permissible to torture slaves to make them give evidence.

Legacy of Roman government

Many modern governments are based on the Roman model. The founders of the United States adopted several Roman ideas in their Constitution. Words such as *"republic," "senate,"* and *"capitol"* are all taken directly from Rome. The idea of an empire with its own religious leader can also be found in the Roman Catholic Church.

Abraham Lincoln was President of the United States from 1861 to 1865.

Elect a government

You can hold your own elections at school for some of the positions of Roman government. Two *consuls* must be appointed to control the Senate and command the armies. Four *aediles* are needed to look after streets, markets, and public buildings, and to organize public games. There are also 20 financial administrators, called *quaestores*, and eight *praetores*, or senior judges. Finally, two *censores* were elected every five years to oversee any changes in the membership of the Senate.

Caligula's horse

Caligula ruled Rome from A.D. 37-41. After a few months as Emperor, he suffered from an illness that affected his mind. He claimed to be a god, and made his horse a senator!

BUILDING FEATS

The Romans were superb engineers and architects and many of their buildings survive today. They include bridges and aqueducts, public baths and, of course, roads. By A.D. 200, the Roman army had built an amazing 53,000 miles of roads. Roads were essential for moving the army quickly around the Empire. They also became important trade routes. The first main road, the Via Appia, was built in 312 B.C., and stretched from Rome to Capua. The Romans also built sewers and central heating systems (see page 13), and invented the first type of concrete. It was made from volcanic rocks and rubble.

A classical style
Roman architecture was heavily influenced by the Greeks. The Romans excelled at building on a grand scale. They used columns, arches, vaults, and domes to create an impression of physical perfection and visual splendor. Architects still use the Roman classical style for buildings like the one below in London, England.

Roman roads took the shortest, straightest route between two places. They were built in layers of crushed stones and gravel, with stone blocks on top. The road had a slight curve, called a camber, and ditches so that rainwater could drain away.

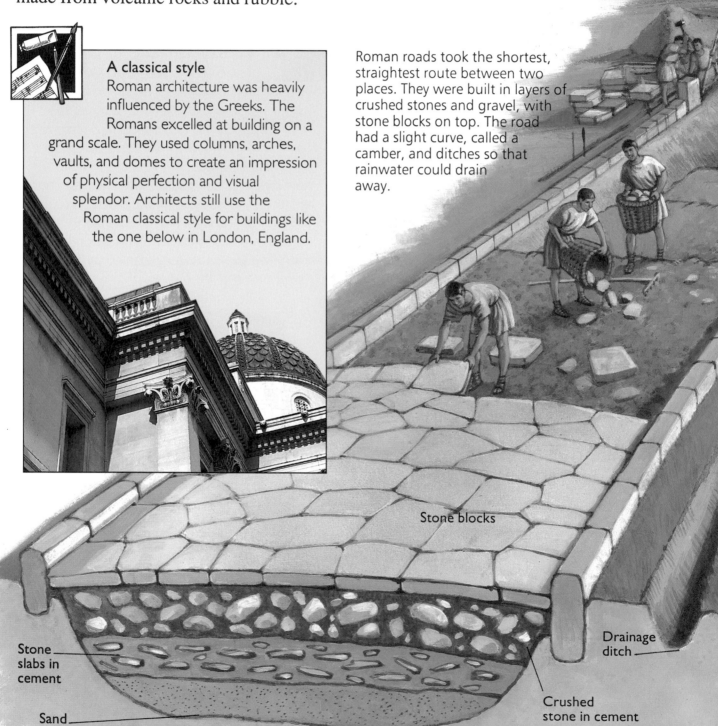

Stone blocks

Stone slabs in cement

Sand

Drainage ditch

Crushed stone in cement

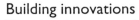

The word mile comes from *mille*, the Latin word for thousand. A Roman mile was 1,000 paces (4,920 feet).

Hot air

Building innovations

The development of the arch enabled the Romans to build many of their famous bridges and aqueducts. Arches were extremely heavy and had to be supported by pillars and buttresses. This helped to distribute their weight, and made the arches incredibly strong. They were built from whatever stone was available. For important buildings, marble was used. The development of concrete made from sand, stone, and water meant that huge, multistoried buildings such as the Colosseum could be built.

Stones

Wooden frame

A cutaway of the Colosseum

Hot baths

Few Roman houses had bathrooms, so people went to the public baths. Here they could bathe, have a massage and chat to their friends. The baths were heated from underground. Slaves stoked large fires which sent hot air under the raised floors and through slits in the walls. The natural hot springs at Bath, England (shown above) were believed to have medicinal properties. People still use the baths for their health-giving properties.

Town planning

Roman towns were built on a grid pattern. At the center of each town was a forum (marketplace), a basilica (town hall) and several temples to the numerous Roman gods. Around the town a holy boundary was marked by massive walls. Outside the city, the roads were lined with gravestones, as burials were forbidden within the holy boundary.

RICH AND POOR

Family life was very important to the Romans. The father was head of the household and was called *paterfamilias*, the "father of the family." The daily running of the house was left to the women. They were not encouraged to go out to work, but instead were expected to raise the children and attend to the domestic duties. There were huge differences between the daily lives of rich and poor in the Roman Empire. Poor city people lived in crowded blocks of apartments, called *insulae*. Most rich Romans had both a city home, called a *domus*, and a country house.

Wealthy housing

The walls and floors of a *domus* were often decorated with beautiful mosaics and frescoes, although there was not much furniture. Lamps burning olive oil provided light.

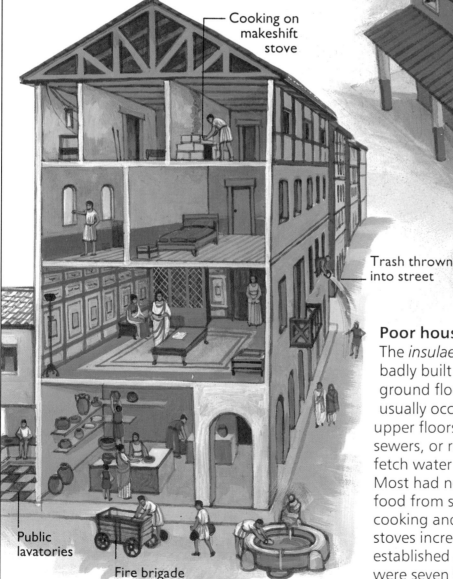

Cooking on makeshift stove

Trash thrown into street

Impluvium

Atrium

Shop

Public lavatories

Fire brigade

Poor housing

The *insulae* of the poor were badly built fire hazards. The ground floor of the *insulae* were usually occupied by a row of shops. The upper floors usually had no heating, sewers, or running water. People had to fetch water from fountains in the street. Most had no kitchen. People bought hot food from shops. Furtive attempts at cooking and heating using wood-burning stoves increased the threat of fire. Augustus established a fire service in Rome. There were seven brigades, called *vigiles*, with 1,000 men in each.

After lunch

Everyone, whether rich or poor, stopped for lunch at noon. Lunch was followed by a short rest, called a siesta, which is still taken in many Mediterranean countries. The wealthy did not work after lunch. Their afternoons consisted of relaxing at the baths and meeting friends. They often invited people home for a long, leisurely meal in the evening.

The poor people worked until dusk, then ate dinner and went to bed when it got dark.

Strigilis

At the baths, strigilis (above) were used for scraping oil and dirt off the skin.

Wealthy women often spent their days reading (right).

— Shrine to household gods

Feasting

Small windows to prevent burglaries

Crime and punishment

Assassinations, pickpocketing, and burglaries were common during the empire. The streets of Rome were policed by groups of men under the control of the city prefect. Criminals were divided into two categories: *honestiores* and *humiliores*. *Humiliores* were usually poorer and given the worst punishments. Offenders could be exiled, or forced to work under harsh conditions.

The message on this mosaic reads: Beware of the dog!

Food and feasting

Wealthy Romans sometimes held lavish feasts for their guests. On the menu there were numerous small dishes, such as eggs, lettuce, snails, or oysters. There may also have been delicacies like lark or dormouse, with plenty of olives, wine, and figs. The Romans did not use cutlery. Guests ate with their hands, which were then wiped by slaves. Wine was mixed with water and drunk out of glass or silver goblets. Honey was added to food and wine to sweeten it.

People reclined on three couches arranged around a table in the *triclinium* (dining room). Nine was the ideal number for a dinner party, with three people on each couch. One end of the table was left clear to allow servants to enter.

ENTERTAINMENT

Public games, paid for by the emperor or wealthy politicians, were an important part of Roman life. There were three main types of "games" (which were known as *ludi* in Latin) - gladiator fights and wild beast shows, chariot races, and theater plays. In Rome, gladiator fights were held in the Colosseum. They were hugely popular. People flocked to watch men armed only with nets and tridents, small shields, or light armor, fight each other to the death. Gladiators were usually slaves or criminals.

A deadly sport

Gladiator fights were usually held in the afternoon. To add to the excitement, fights were held between different types of gladiator. For example, a *retiarius*, armed with only a trident and a weighted net might fight a samnite with a shield and a sword or spear. A wounded gladiator could appeal for mercy. If the crowd put their thumbs up, he was spared. Thumbs down, and he was killed.

Fun and games

The games played by Roman children were similar to those played today. A game like marbles was played with walnuts. *Tali* (knucklebones) was played with pieces of pottery and was similar to dice. Board games were also popular. Make a Roman version of the board game Ludo based on a chariot race. Use different colored counters for the teams.

Marbles and walnuts

Whip top

Knuckle-bones (tali)

One of the highlights of a day at the Games was the beast show (minera). Rich Romans hunted throughout the provinces of the Empire and beyond for rare and exotic animals. At great expense, antelopes, elephants, Indian tigers, and rhinos were shipped back to Rome to fight in the arena. The animals were forced to fight each other or were pitted against unarmed criminals. Thousands of animals and humans died in these violent and bloody battles.

The circus Maximus

In Rome, chariot races were held in the huge Circus Maximus. There were four teams – the Reds, Greens, Blues, and Whites. People supported their own team with great passion and often placed money on the outcome! A race consisted of as many as 12 chariots running seven laps of the tracks (a distance of about 5 miles). Drivers had to be extremely skillful to keep the horses under control. "Naval battles" were also held in the Circus Maximus and the arena was specially flooded for this purpose.

Making music

Music and dancing were important aspects of Roman culture, and took place at the theater, public games, and some religious festivals. Competitions were even held during intervals at the amphitheater to find the person who could blow the longest note! Many Roman instruments were of Greek origin, and can be recognized in our instruments today. Lyres, below, were very popular with the Romans and were often associated with the gods.

"The Music Lesson," a first century wall painting from Herculaneum, Italy.

Theater masks

All the parts in a Roman play were played by male actors, even the female roles! To help the audience distinguish between the different characters, the actors wore masks on stage. Try making a Roman theater mask from papier mâché. Decorate your mask according to the type of character you are playing, with a smiling face for comedy and a sad face for tragedy.

GODS AND RELIGION

The Romans worshiped a great many gods and spirits – about 30,000 in all. These included the major gods and goddesses, such as Jupiter, the chief god, Neptune, god of the sea, Venus, goddess of love and beauty, and Minerva, goddess of wisdom and war. Each household also worshipped its own protective spirits – the Lares, Penates, and Manes. After Augustus's death, the emperors were considered gods, too. People all over the empire were allowed to worship their own local gods, as long as they also paid homage to the Roman gods. Large and impressive temples, often modeled on Greek examples, were built as places of worship for the state deities.

One of the household Lares; the guardian of houses.

Household gods

Every Roman house had its own shrine to the household gods (Lares), called a Lararium, where worship was carried out daily. The family offered gifts such as wine, bread, and fruit, and also gave sacrifices to the gods. Outside the home, people worshipped the Roman gods in shrines and temples (right).

Festivals

Roman festivals were regarded as holy days (holidays), during which people did not have to work.

Under Augustus there were about 130 public holidays, and this number increased under later emperors. The festivals were usually celebrated with games and races.

Compitalia occurred in early January. Farmers built a shrine and made sacrifices to ensure the prosperity of their farms. During *Parilia*, in April, people danced around a bonfire onto which offerings were thrown.

The Rites of Bona Dea was held in early December. The festival was for women only, and men were forbidden to attend.

Religious persecution
During the empire, many Romans felt the empty rituals of the state religion could no longer meet their spiritual needs. Foreign cults such as those of Mithras, Isis, and Cybele encouraged their followers to take part in ceremonies, and spread across the empire. Christianity was not tolerated by the Romans, however. Its followers refused to worship the state gods and were often cruelly persecuted.

Vestals
Vesta was the goddess of the hearth. The six Vestal virgins had to perform symbolic household duties for the state. This included tending the fire dedicated to Vesta which burned in her temple in the forum. The virgins had to remain unmarried for 30 years. Those who did not were buried alive.

Offerings and sacrifices
People tried to discover the will of the gods with sacrifices. Sheep, chickens, bulls, and pigs were the main sacrificial animals. The priests removed their innards and read them to discover the gods' intentions.

Looking heavenward
The positions of the stars and the planets at the time of a person's birth were considered very significant by the Romans.

Mercury

Ceremonies
Special ceremonies marked important events in the lives of all Romans. A newborn baby was placed at its father's feet. The father raised the child in his arms as a sign of acceptance into the family. Funerals were very grand affairs, with professional mourners hired to wail over the body. In Republican times, death masks and mourning robes were worn. This practice was stopped during the empire.

Jupiter

Many of the stars and planets were named after Roman and Greek gods and goddesses. For example, Mercury was named after the messenger of the gods, who was also the god of trade and thieves. Venus was the goddess of love and beauty and Mars was the god of war. Jupiter was the king of the gods – the god of thunder and of lightning. Can you find out who the other planets were named after?

Roman marriages were usually arranged. The couple clasped hands (shown right) as a symbol of their marriage.

Venus

THE ROMAN LANGUAGE

The Romans spoke a language called Latin. It provided a common language across the empire, and enabled people from far and wide to communicate with each other about matters such as trade and government. Greek was also widely spoken in the east. Many of our everyday words come from Latin origins and the alphabet used in western Europe is based on the Latin alphabet below. During the Middle Ages, Latin was the main language of the Church and scholarship. It remained the official language of the Roman Catholic Church well into this century.

A B C D E F G H I J K M

N O P Q R S T U V W X Y

Schooling

Only children whose parents could afford it received an education.

From the age of six, Roman boys attended a kind of primary school called a *ludus*. Rich children were accompanied by a slave called a pedagogue, who supervised the child throughout the school day. Although most children left school at 11, the wealthy ones went on to attend a secondary school, or *grammaticus*.

Young boys stayed with their mothers until they were old enough to go to school. Girls also stayed at home, where they were taught skills such as weaving and spinning by their mothers.

Here, one of the main aims was to prepare teenage boys for a life in politics, the law, or public speaking. Girls received only a very basic education, after which they learned how to be wives and mothers.

Writers and poets

There were many famous Roman writers and poets, such as Vergil, Livy, Cicero, Catullus, and Pliny. One of the most famous Roman works is Vergil's epic poem, *Aeneid* (illustrated right). It is the story of Aeneas, a legendary Trojan hero. When Troy was destroyed by the Greeks, Aeneas escaped to Italy, where his descendants founded Rome.

Writing

Writing at school was done on a piece of wood that was covered with wax. A pointed metal stick, called a stylus, was used to scratch letters and figures onto the wax. To make a writing tablet, chop up several candles into a bowl. Melt the wax over a pot of boiling water (get an adult to help you with this), and pour it into a shallow tray. Let it cool. Use a knitting needle point or blunt pencil to write on your tablet.

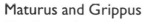

Maturus and Grippus

The lives of wealthy and poor children were very different. Maturus is poor and Grippus is rich. In diary form, describe what a day in the life of each boy would be like. For example, if Maturus is poor, he will not be able to read and write. Describe a visit to the market, where Maturus has to buy his dinner. What is his home like? Grippus, on the other hand, is educated. Who takes him to school every day? What kinds of things does he learn at school? And what games does he play when the school day finishes?

Genus

Latin names are used for scientific classifications. Below are some Latin names used in natural history.

The genus (group) Equus consists of horses, asses, and zebra. The word equestrian, meaning horsemanship, comes from this group name.

Felix is the Latin name for the cat family. From it comes the word feline, which means cat-like.

Bovis is the Latin term for cattle. Today, the word bovine means resembling cows.

THE END OF THE EMPIRE

Toward the end of the second century A.D., the Roman Empire began to face problems. Barbarian tribes started invading Roman territory. The army grew weaker and could not control the worsening situation. At home, rival emperors squabbled over power. In A.D. 285, Emperor Diocletian divided the empire into two parts – west and east, each with its own emperor. But rising prices and taxes, and increasing invasions led to collapse in the west. In A.D. 476, the last western emperor, Romulus Augustulus, was deposed. The eastern empire, known as the Byzantine Empire, continued to flourish, however.

Angles, Jutes and Saxons
The Angles, Saxons, and Jutes moved into and took over the Roman provinces in Britain.

Burgundians
The Burgundians were from Northern Europe. In A.D. 406, they set up their own kingdom in Germania.

Visigoths
The Visigoths settled in Dacia in the A.D. 200s. In A.D. 410, led by the Goth chief, Alaric, they sacked the city of Rome.

The Lombards
In A.D. 568 the Lombards conquered Northern Italy and set up the kingdom of Lombardy.

Franks
The Franks invaded Gaul, giving their names to modern-day France.

Huns
The Huns came from eastern Asia. They invaded the lands of the Vandals, Ostrogoths, and Visigoths.

 ROMAN EMPIRE

Vandals
The Vandals were of Scandinavian descent. In A.D. 409, they took control of Roman provinces in North Africa and Spain.

Ostrogoths
In the A.D. 370s, the Ostrogoths moved westward to escape the Huns. They overran Italy in A.D. 489.

Overspending
Toward the end of the Empire, vast sums of money were spent on lavish projects and games, which led to massive inflation. The currency collapsed, prices rose, and taxation was heavy. Coins minted at this time lost their value so quickly that new ones of higher values had to be minted. Many poverty-stricken people were forced to abandon their homes and often joined bands of outlaws.

The coming of Christianity

In the 4th century A.D., the Christian Church became more powerful and began to influence the way the empire was run. When the barbarians started invading, it was Christian bishops, not army generals, who mostly organized the defense against them.

This mosaic is in the church of St. Sophia, Istanbul.

Civil wars

During the 3rd century A.D., it became clear that the empire could no longer be effectively controlled from a central authority in Rome. A series of civil wars erupted between A.D. 235-284, which drastically weakened the army's power. Struggles among army generals for control of the empire further weakened the empire's defenses. When Rome was attacked from the east by the newly-formed and powerful Persian Empire, and from the north by the Germans, the collapse of the Roman Empire seemed inevitable.

The remains of the empire

The Emperor Constantine began reuniting the empire after its split into east and west by Diocletian. In A.D. 330, Constantine moved his court from Rome to Byzantium. There, he founded a new capital city to rival the former power and splendor of Rome. It was called Constantinople (modern-day Istanbul). The Byzantine Empire survived until A.D. 1453, when Constantinople was finally captured by the Turks.

Roman remains in modern-day Turkey

THE LEGACY OF ROME

Even today, over 1,500 years after the decline of the empire, Rome still has an enormous influence over our lives. Many of our buildings were copied from the Roman style of architecture. Our legal and political systems can be traced back to Roman times. In addition, there is a huge quantity of historical evidence, from literature and coins, to surviving roads and aqueducts, to keep the memory of Rome well and truly alive.

The Radcliffe Camera is a library in Oxford, England. Its architect, James Gibbs (1683-1754), modeled it on a Roman basilica. The dome, the pillars, and the ornate, classical style are reminiscent of many of the magnificent buildings of the Roman Empire. Several major cities have been built on sites chosen by the Romans. For example, Londinium (modern day London) was founded by the Romans in A.D. 43 as a seaport. Can you find out any other examples of towns or cities which were built by the Romans, and which remain today?

The Roman revival
In the early 15th century, writers, artists, sculptors, and architects began to draw inspiration from ancient Greece and Rome. Ruins were studied and statues were dug up. Ancient myths and legends were used as the basis for paintings, such as the French artist Claude's depiction of Aeneas at Delos (shown right). Latin literature also provided inspiration for Renaissance writers. The English poet Pope was greatly influenced by the Latin writer Juvenal throughout his work.

The European Community flag

The period of Roman Empire demonstrated the possibility of one government controlling large areas. Roman citizenship·gave people a sense of identity. Today the European Community can be seen to reflect Roman ideals of unity, albeit with modern goals of a single monetary and taxation system, and a central government.

Herbal medicine

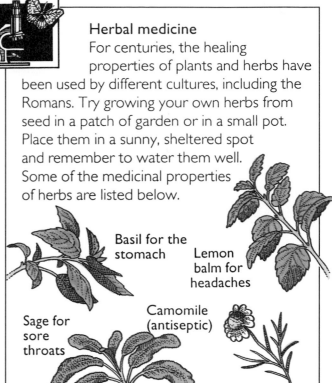

For centuries, the healing properties of plants and herbs have been used by different cultures, including the Romans. Try growing your own herbs from seed in a patch of garden or in a small pot. Place them in a sunny, sheltered spot and remember to water them well. Some of the medicinal properties of herbs are listed below.

Basil for the stomach

Lemon balm for headaches

Sage for sore throats

Camomile (antiseptic)

Pompeii

Much of the evidence that we have today about ancient Rome comes from archaeological excavations such as Pompeii (below). The town has been well preserved under the volcanic ash and lava which engulfed it in A.D. 79. Its forum, basilica, theaters, temples, lavish villas, and tiny sleeping quarters offer a complete picture of Roman life. The ruins also provide us with a valuable insight into many aspects of Roman civilization and culture.

The archaeological remains of Pompeii, which was destroyed by the volcano, Vesuvius, in A.D. 79.

The French Empire

The Imperial system used by the Romans was later copied by rulers of other European countries. The Frankish king, Charlemagne, revived the idea of the Roman Empire in the West. It was termed the Holy Roman Empire by subsequent Frankish and German leaders. The Holy Roman Empire was destroyed by Napoleon Bonaparte who modeled his own empire on that of Rome and even called himself emperor.

753 B.C. Traditional date for the founding of Rome

510 Last king expelled from Rome; Republic formed

49 Caesar returns to Rome and seizes power; civil war breaks out

31 Victory for Octavian at the Battle of Actium

27 Octavian becomes the first emperor and the Roman Empire begins

0 (Actual birth of Christ c. 5 B.C.)

A.D. 14 Augustus dies

43 Roman conquest of southern Britain

117 Death of Trajan; accession of Hadrian. Roman Empire at its greatest extent

212 Roman citizenship granted to all free members of the empire

230s onward Wars with Persia. Barbarians begin invasions across Rhine and Danube

253-268 Germanic barbarians invade the empire

284 Accession of Diocletian, who splits empire into East and West

312 Constantine becomes emperor. Reunites empire from 324 onward

313 Edict of Milan. Christianity tolerated within empire

410 Rome captured by Alaric the Goth; around this time, Roman rule ends in Britain

476 Romulus Augustulus, last western Roman Emperor is deposed by Odovacar, a barbarian leader

8000 B.C.

First hieroglyphs (picture writing) in Egypt c.3500 B.C.

Old Kingdom in Egypt 2628-2181 B.C.

Pyramids built in Egypt during Old Kingdom

Egyptian Middle Kingdom 2181-1567 B.C.

2000 B.C.

Tutankhamun -the boy pharaoh 1361-1237 B.C.

New Kingdom in Egypt 1567-1085 B.C.

Romulus and Remus found the city of Rome 753 B.C.

500 B.C.

Roman Empire c.27 B.C.-c.A.D. 476

Julius Caesar murdered 44 B.C.

Fall of the Roman Empire A.D. 476

Viking raids on Britain and France A.D. 793-1000

A.D.1000

First Crusade to recapture Holy Land from Muslims A.D.1096

First mechanical clock developed

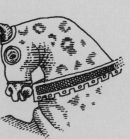

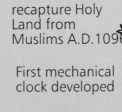

The Aztec Empire in Central America A.D. 1300-1521

A.D. 1350-1532 Growth of the Inca Empire in South America

8000-5650 B.C.
First cities – Jericho and Catal Hüyük

3500-3000 B.C.
Wheel invented by the Sumerians

2500-1500 B.C.
Rise of the Indus Valley civilization

Early Minoan period in Crete begins c.2500 B.C.

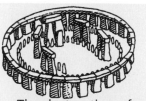

Stonehenge completed in England c.1500 B.C.

The destruction of Knossos in Crete. End of the Minoan period c.1200 B.C.

c.500 B.C. Life of Gautama the Buddha

c.1400-1027 B.C. Shang dynasty in China.

Birth of Confucius 551 B.C.

The Golden Age of Greece 478-405 B.C.

Alexander the Great conquers Persia, Syria, and Eygpt 331 B.C.

The first Empire in China 221 B.C.-A.D. 618

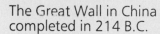

The Great Wall in China completed in 214 B.C.

Samurai warriors of Japan from A.D. 1100-1850

The Plague, or Black Death, spread throughout Europe A.D. 1347.

First mechanical printing press developed by Gutenberg in Germany in A.D. 1455

Christopher Columbus sets sail for the West Indies and became the first European to discover America.

GLOSSARY

Aediles Roman government officials who looked after the streets, markets, and public buildings.

Augustus The honorary title given to the Emperor. It means "revered" in Latin.

Basilica A large public building, used as a town hall or law courts.

Censores Government officials, elected every five years to revise the Senate membership.

Centurion The officer in charge of an army unit, called a century. A century was made up of 100, and later 80 men.

Consul The most senior official in the government. Two *consuls* were elected each year by the Senate. They controlled the Senate and commanded the Roman army.

Equites Rich business people, including merchants, bankers, and traders.

Forum A large open space in the center of a Roman town. It doubled as a market place and meeting place.

Insulae Blocks of apartments in Roman towns and cities.

Legion An army unit. It was made up of about 5,000 soldiers, or legionaries.

Mosaic A pattern or picture made of tiny pieces of tile or glass.

Paterfamilias The head of a Roman family. The father.

Patricians The richest, most aristocratic Romans.

Pax Romana The "Roman Peace." A time of peace and prosperity under Emperors Trajan and Hadrian.

Plebeians Ordinary Romans; the common people.

Praetores Government officials who acted as senior judges.

Quaestores Government officials in charge of financial administration.

Senate The council of citizens that ruled Rome.

INDEX

Aeneid 25
Agrippina 7
arches 17
architecture 16, 17, 28
army 8-10
Augustus 6, 7, 12, 22, 31

barbarian tribes 26, 27
baths 17, 19
beast show 20
building 16, 17, 22, 28
Byzantium 27, 28

Caligula 7
Carthage 4, 5
central heating 13, 16
chariot races 21
Christianity 12, 23, 24, 27
citizens 10, 11
civil wars 4-6, 27
classes 11, 18
coinage 12, 26
Constantine 27
consuls 5, 31

Diocletian 26, 27
Domitian 7
domus 18

emperors 6, 7, 14, 22
entertainment 20, 21
equites 11, 31

families 10, 18, 19
farming 5, 7
festivals 5, 19, 22, 23

forum 17, 31

games 20, 21
gladiator fights 20
gods 13, 22, 23
government 6, 10, 14, 15, 28, 29
Greece 5, 11, 16, 24

Hadrian 7, 12, 13
Hadrian's Wall 13
Hannibal 4
Holy Roman Empire 29
housing 18, 19

insulae 18, 31

Julian calendar 5
Julius Caesar 5-7
Justinian Code 14

language 24, 25
law 14, 28
legions 8, 9, 31

Marius, General 8
medicine 13, 17, 29
mosaics 13, 31

Napoleon 29
Nero 7
numerals 12

Octavian 6

Parthenon 5

patricians 11, 31
Pax Romana 12, 13, 31
Persian e27
plebeians 11, 14, 31
Pompeii 29
Punic Wars 4, 5

religion 13, 22, 23
Republic 4, 5, 10, 14
roads 16
Rome 4, 27
Romulus and Remus 4
Romulus Augustulus 26

sacrifices 23
Saturnalia 5
schools 24
Senate 4, 5, 10, 14, 31
slaves 5, 10, 11, 19, 20
society 10, 11
Spartacus 11

temples 22
theater masks 21
Tiberius 7
Titus 7
toga 10
tortoise technique 9
town planning 17
trade 11, 12
Trajan 7, 12
trials 14

Vespasian 7
Vergil 25
vestal virgins 23

Photographic credits:
All pictures taken by Roger Vlitos apart from: back cover top left and right, 6, 12 top and middle left, 18, 19 top right and bottom right, 20, 21 left and 23: Trustees of the British Museum, 4 top, 5 top right, 22-23 and 25 top: Hulton Picture Company; 4 bottom, 5 bottom, 11, 24 bottom, 26 top and 27 top: Mary Evans; 5 top left and 22 top: Eye Ubiquitous; 9, 12 middle right 15, 17, 22 bottom and 27 bottom left: Spectrum; 10 bottom no.4 and 27 bottom right: Frank Spooner Pictures; 12 bottom, 25 bottom, 28 middle and 29 bottom left: Robert Harding; 13 middle and 22 middle: Michael Holford; 28 bottom: Reproduced by courtesy of the Trustees, The National Gallery, London; 29 top and bottom right: Paul Nightingale.